BREAK FREE AND LEARN TO TRADE

RAT TRAP: BREAK FREE AND LEARN TO TRADE

Tools to take back your financial independence and grow your own investment or retirement account.

James E. Brown, PhD

TABLE OF CONTENTS

A smart man makes a mistake, learns from it, and never makes that mistake again. But a wise man finds a smart man and learns from him how to avoid the mistake altogether.

~ Roy H. Williams ~

DEDICATION

I dedicate this book to the frustrated, fed up, and lost but still hopeful retirees, private investors, and intermediate traders. May this book find you at the right time and place in your lives and trading journey. If this book reaches and helps one person become a better trader, I deem it a success.

PREFACE

What made you preview or purchase this book? Are you looking for the holy grail of trading? Are you frustrated with your strategy and looking for improvements? Are you on the hamster wheel and rat race of indicator purchases?

Whatever difficulties and pain have brought you to this point, you are not alone. You have recognized the most important step. Recognizing the point of pain.

"No one cares about your trading story until you are making money!" In planning this book, I heard those very words. No one cares about your story; people only care about what you can give them.

Shocked, but thinking like a reader in search of a million-dollar strategy, I wrote a book focused on helping traders understand the nuances of the market.

It offers the truth as I see it, and only gives the tools necessary for potential success and nothing else, which would cause this book to be short in scope. The goal is to add value to the trader and have the reader learn something new that will add to their overall success in this business.

I have over 10 years of trading experience. Over the years, I have been through both the massive gut-punching losses and the exhilarating wins.

As a trader, these trading wins and losses have taken a serious toll on my health and trading behavior. I have tried different tools to combat this issue from turning off the computer for a few days to relaxing and choosing to stop listening to trading strategies from various "gurus."

This book is the basics of wave trading. Looking at the basic tools needed to earn a profit when engaging if all factors are aligned and intact.

The goals of this book are to have the trader:

Strip down complexities in trading and apply basics. Getting to what is real.

Calm the emotions of frustrated traders.

Shorten the learning curve and shave years off the learning experience.

Save thousands of dollars in lost revenue.

Stop going down the indicator and course purchas- ing rabbit hole.

To begin trading once you finish this book. Empower you with the basic tools needed to succeed.

I do not intend this book to be a get rich quick tool or the final authority on this trading philosophy.

As you progress through the book, I will present tools to assist in your trading journey. These will likely differ from what you attempted before but do try them.

The book does not explain:

Opening an account

Navigating through the trading platform Adding or removing indicators on charts Futures basics

Broker types

Futures clearing firm (FCM) Margins, commissions, contracts

While beginners will enjoy the concepts of this book; this book was written with the intermediate trader in the futures market in mind. If you buy this book, I am to assume that you have six months or more trading experience. Trader's with the minimum experience and has prior knowledge in wave trading, this book is not for you.

Ultimately, I believe there is a direct link between a successful trader and the ability to manage a SOUND MIND, SOUND METHOD, and SOUND MONEY, but it all starts with a sound mind. Without the proper mindset and discipline, you will not be a successful trader. This book will help you develop the skill, the mindset, and the motivation to take your trading to the next level.

Let's get started.

ACKNOWLEDGMENTS

My wife Kim, my cheerleader, who has been there from the very start—watching me fall, pick myself up to only fall again. Watching me obsess over the market through late nights and early mornings. You have never once judged and only given me words of support to continue on with my dream if it made me happy. I love you.

To Toni Becker, my spiritual teacher, and dear friend. Words cannot do justice to how you open my eyes to new ways to view the spiritual world and how you shined the light while I was in a dark place. When we met while I was in undergraduate studies, I did not realize that the journey would make me a part of your family. Again, words cannot do justice to the love and kindness you give. Thank you.

To Damian Castilla, my mentor. When I was at my lowest during my trading journey, you arrived at the right time. As a full-time trader, you would take the time out to show me "what is real" and held me responsible and accountable for all my decisions and actions and made me own them. While everyone else charges enormous fees for the "secret sauce," you taught out of sheer kindness and a philosophy of "Paying it forward." It created this book. I aligned my process, and you showed me the true way to look at trading. I thank you.

RISKS ASSOCIATED WITH TRADING

RISK DISCLOSURE: Futures, foreign currency, and options trading contains substantial risk and are not for every investor. Risk capital is money that can be lost without jeopardizing one's financial security or lifestyle. Only risk capital should be used for trading and only those with sufficient risk capital should trade.

Past performance is not indicative of future results.

Trading can be a challenging and profitable opportunity for investors. However, before taking part in any market, contemplate your investment objectives, level of experience, and risk appetite. Do not invest money you cannot afford to lose.

There is considerable exposure to risk in any transaction. Every transaction involving securities involves risks, including but not limited to the potential for changing political and/or economic conditions that may affect the price or liquidity of a security. Investments in speculation may also be susceptible to sharp rises and fall as the market values fluctuate.

1
PSYCHOLOGY & PERSONALITY

"We are addicted to our thoughts. We change nothing if we cannot change our thinking."

~ Santosh ftalwar ~

Behavior mindset

A trader's decision-making process, personality, and inner self reveals through trading wins, losses, and breakeven.

Personality and negative habits developed over the years are clear when traders take this journey. A blown account drudges up feeling from past unresolved and unrelated to trading—feelings of fear, greed, anger, confusion and many others.

True acceptance and knowledge of self correlate to a sound decision-making process, a change in trading behavior, and change in world perspective.

As traders, we all have earned PhDs and had the same learning curve from the school of hard knocks. No trader is exempt from this. This defines a trader; it has molded us.

The goal is to shorten the curve for the next generation and take time to focus on starting with a small account size while learning.

To understand your true nature and to assess a trader's mindset, then real money must be on the line. Get some skin in the game.

By working on developing your mindset and working the method, you will be establishing the greatest foundation for success.

Conditioned Mindset

Moving from an unsuccessful trader to a successful trader is to accept and shift the mindset responsible for the actions of losses; brought on by fear or greed.

The behavior of traders consists of learned habits that implanted themselves into our mindset as children.

Regarding fear, according to the Merriam-Webster dictionary, fear is an unpleasant often strong emotion caused by anticipation or awareness of danger.

Fear is brought about from a known or unknown source produces stress, a physical, chemical, or emotional factor that causes tension in the body.

Fear is an adaptive behavior or "condition response." Ivan Pavlov studied this behavior, and Burrhus Frederic Skinner later built upon this research.

In his work, Skinner conducted research on rats to determine a connection between stimuli and observable behavior in rats.

Rats were enclosed in a box with levers, electrified floors, and food allowing for the measurement and control of certain conditions.

The purpose was to predict consequences, rewards, and punishments. The research used a model where an unfavorable decision resulted in punishment, and a correct decision resulted in a reward. By breaking tasks down into smaller parts, and rewarding success on those parts, Skinner facilitated behavioral change in animals (Skinner, 1960).

What Skinner did was significant. He felt humans did not differ from rats and would learn adjusted behavior through graded steps with feedback at each stage. His views on behavioral change applied to human actions have driven an entire field of behavior modification.

Fear & Greed Mindset

When fear is brought upon us by an unknown circumstance, it often impedes our decision-making process. When a trade is open, traders venture into the unknown.

Even though a trading method is in place, traders relinquish con- trol and must trust the outcome will be favorable. If not, a trader will then punish themselves by scrutinizing trades and negative behavior might surface.

We have many trading emotions, but fear and greed are the two biggest. Having a positive attitude brings a positive expectancy, and a decisive trader trades despite fear.

The trader accepts the possibility of losses or mistakes yet has the confidence to take action despite fear and greed.

To take full advantage of the journey, traders must define them- selves.

"To know thyself is the beginning of wisdom."
~ Socrates ~

Trader

What defines a trader and the ability to use the mindset and method to engage the market? It begins with the identity of self, and the ability to use the right method to align with a trader character type.

Are you trading this way? Does your method correlate with your trading style and personality?

Traders start their trading journey searching for a trading system first and not led to ask the tough questions within them.

Before introspection, traders find a method which makes money. It is only when it stops making money that we begin to question the process. "It was working before, but why did it stop?" So, we move on to a new method and similar results happen again. Then the hamster wheel cycle begins.

As traders, the goal is to remember successful repetitions develop into successful habits, developed by following the system as designed and implemented.

What classifies a successful trader? Ability to follow an established plan and not lead based on emotion. For instance, getting into a position after a candle closes versus getting in before.

When small wins occur, take note to understand how the win happened and what state of mind you were in. This documentation is key to future wins.

Traits

We vary in shapes, sizes, colors, religions, cultures, beliefs, even our personalities. This adds to our uniqueness and individuality.

People come to trading from all backgrounds and walks of life in search of intellectual stimulation, employment or to find riches beyond their wildest dreams. With this, each trader brings their own personalities, egos, and ideas about how they view the market.

This is the main reason why there are different classifications and types of traders. Trading is different for each person and each has specific needs.

Individuation

Carl Jung, a psychiatrist, and psychoanalyst created analytical psychology and individuation. The main concept of individuation is knowing self and how the individual's conscious (see) and unconscious (hidden) selves merge.

He understood the complexities of the human psyche and the need for an individualized approach. Traders are all specialized individuals.

There is an obvious truth, traders are not looking for a psycholo- gy lesson, but it's about what a trader needs not what they want if they want to move forward. This information gives a clue about the origination and creation of the mindset.

Carl Jung believes there are three sides to the total personality: the persona, the shadow, and the self. We will focus on persona and shadow.

Persona

This concept refers to the role people play each day. A mask. We will peel this layer back first with this story.

As a teenager, Julie lived in a small town in Podunk, Alabama, with only two streetlights. She had a picture of New York City on her wall and had big dreams of becoming a dancer. She was a very talented dancer. When she graduated from high school and was accepted to The School of Music and Dance, her dreams came true. Excited to arrive in the big city, Julie hid her Alabama accent so no one would make fun of her. Her first semester was a success and in the summer, she went home to see her grandparents and enjoy the comforts of home. When around family, her Alabama accent came out.

Shadow

The shadow is something people hide from the world; it is the repressed emotions from one's life. It is from trauma or elicited negative feedback from others.

We push trauma down to the unconscious where a shadow forms. The shadow is another side of ourselves and it is its own entity. To correct, it must be acknowledged and addressed.

Do you remember Julie from Podunk, Alabama? There is more to the story. Julie was born in Chickasaw, Alabama to a very abusive alcoholic single mother. During times of stress, Julie would run to her favorite spot to dance and think of a world better than her own. Julie knew how to repress the pain at an early age through dance. After her mother died of alcohol poisoning, she moved to Podunk, Alabama to live with her grandparents. While this gave her a new start, the shadows of hurt, neglect, abuse, escapism, self-esteem issues, lack of belonging rooted themselves inside of her.

What is the takeaway? We all have masks and shadows. When Julie embarked on her journey as a student dancer, she put on her language mask to hide her accent from the world to erase the fact that she was from a small town. When she arrives home, Julie puts on her Alabama mask again.

With her shadow story, the true story lies in why she loves dancing so much. It's because of childhood issues and a way to escape the shadow created by her mother when she was a child.

How does this relate to trading? Trading is yet one more role we must play. We must think of ourselves as successful traders and convince ourselves until it is true. This is only part of the story.

To understand our true selves and our trading habits, we must go into the shadows. Traders experience emotions from trading loss or experience excitement from wins.

Our mindset shifts from an "I'm a loser" to "I'm a winner." Although we move back and forth in our mindset while trading, there is a deeper element to the story.

Successful traders have done and continue to grow as they develop themselves and their trading skills.

This is a trading book and not a course in psychology, but to take advantage of the fullness of trading, it is critical to understand that *knowledge of self and getting a handle on emotional trading is the foundation of trading.* Ask any full-time successful trader. Successful traders must develop and align the right mindset.

Carl Jung said it best:

"Unfortunately, there can be no doubt that man is, on the whole, less good than he imagines himself or wants to be. Everyone carries a shadow, and the less it is embodied in the individual's conscious life, the blacker and denser it is. If an inferiority is conscious, one always has a chance to correct it. But if it is repressed and isolated from conscious, it never gets corrected." (Jung, 1969)

Trader Type Alignment

To pull back the curtain and look in on our trader personality, we require assessments. Assessment is not a conclusive process of getting to the root of personality but it is a starting point.

I have recommended these tests to other traders as a way to give them further confirmation of their strengths and weaknesses, so they can align with the method that works best for them.

The combination of all three tests to identify personality type is a new concept, not an exact science—but it gets us close to an understanding ourselves and habits. Each scholar has various techniques to arrive at a conclusion of trader personality and it is the belief of the writer, that more insight into a trader personality only enhances a trader's knowledge and habits so that growth can begin.

HumanMetrics Myers-Briggs Test

Carl Jung believed to get to the true self we must reach the shadow. Each persons' shadows have a dominant function and a repressive function. Our jobs is to best recognize them and move as close to the center of the true self as we can.

To do this, inspired by Carl Jung's teachings on personality, Isabel Briggs-Myers and Katharine Cook Briggs developed an assessment called the Myers-Briggs Type Indicator test.

Tharp Test

Van K. Tharp a trained psychologist has firsthand experience losing trades. Because of these losses, he researched and noticed certain trader characteristics in investment and trading success.

This led to his detailed trader and investment profile. He also created a mini version of this test, which gives a snapshot of a trader's personality, temperament, perception, and interpretation. He witnessed fifteen trader types.

A.W.A.R. E Test

Kenneth Reid is a clinical psychologist and the developer of the AWARE test based on different personality types. The different types he identified were: Agrarian, Warrior, Artist, Realist, and Engineer. Through this analysis, a trader can see how they fall into one or multiple categories. Below are the results from my own assessment.

James's Trader Alignment Assessment Results

Human Metrics Test

INTJ is known as the "System Builders" of the types, perhaps in part because they possess the unusu- al trait combination of imagination and reliability. Whatever system this type is working on is for them the equivalent of a moral cause to an INTJ, both perfectionism and disregard for authority may come into play, as INJT's can be unsparing of both themselves and others on the project. Anyone considered to be "slacking" including superiors, will lose their respect and will generally be made aware of this; INTJs have also been known to take it upon themselves to implement critical decisions without con- sulting their supervisors or co-workers. But they do be scrupulous and even-handed about recognizing the individual contributors that have gone into a project and have a gift for seizing opportunities which others might not even notice.

Tharp Trader Test

As a <u>Detailed Trader</u>... you earn your success by being thorough, methodical, systematic, organized and dependable. You are also realistic and responsible if things make sense for you. You have two of the three qualities for trading success (i.e. you decide based on logic and analysis and you are decisive, orderly and things sequentially).

Agrarian, Warrior, Artist, Realist, Engineer (A.W.A.R. E)

Personality Test

Most traders express one type but two are not uncommon. As traders develop individuals integrate more approaches called Super Hybrid. Super Hybrid test results are associated with advanced traders. Super Hybrid traders are more successful because they are more adaptive. These traders have matured organ- ically to achieve mastery over the complex market conditions. Your most dominant types are Agrarian, Realist and Engineer.

Agrarian traders *are laid back individuals who take careful, consistent and conservative approach to life and trading. Agrarian traders' consistency is much more important than spontaneity or creativity. Agrarian take a calculated risk and want a clear reliable method they can apply repeat. They take a longer-term perspective which means they are more suited for swing trading than day trading* ***Realist traders*** *approach trading in a practical manner with a focus on works. The realist will be okay trading a Black Box system if it produced results. Winning matter and they will be disappointed in themselves if they don't win. A realist might seek to emulate certain qualities of famous traders and they aspire to that lifestyle.* ***Engineer*** *traders are detailed oriented and rarely make mistakes. Engi- neers are conservative and methodical with risk-taking in trading. Engineer trader relies on reason, not a gut feeling, to succeed. They only take a calculated risk and they can give you the numbers: risk/ reward and other performances.*

Overall Classification: *Based on trader type alignment assessment results, I have a Swing Trader style and will only place trades using the Swing Trade method and plan, which will keep me in trades that will last a day or few days. I will not look at any other trading method that will cause my mindset to shift from a relaxed trader's mindset to a stressful trader's mindset.*

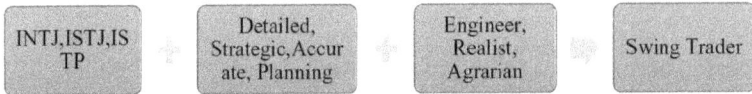

INTJ,ISTJ,IS TP	Detailed, Strategic,Accur ate, Planning	Engineer, Realist, Agrarian	Swing Trader

Now it's your turn to apply the principles to look inward to assess your alignment. Traders must take a solid and honest inventory. Be serious and answer the questions. This will be for your own benefit as a trader.

Completing these tests should help with alignment and trader success. Begin with the HumanMetrics test to determine the four-personality types and apply them to your tailored trading method.

Understanding your decision-making style, trader style, and knowing the reasons why you trade is paramount to a successful trading future.

We seek to achieve a score in each category and lead to align- ment type. What if a trader only achieves results in each cate- gory? The simplest way to know which trader type gives you the least stress is to know your trader's type.

What helps is the analysis of the current career path chosen by you, the trader. This shows personality alignment.

Don't second guess it. Remember the aim is a stable stress-free mindset when trading.

Trader Alignment Chart

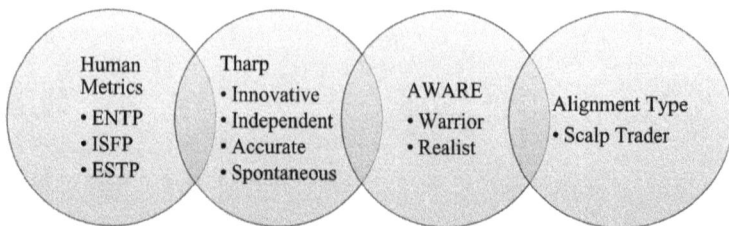

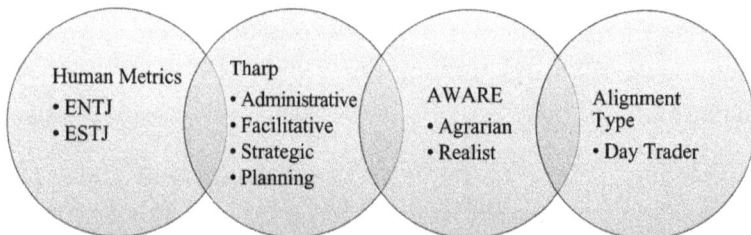

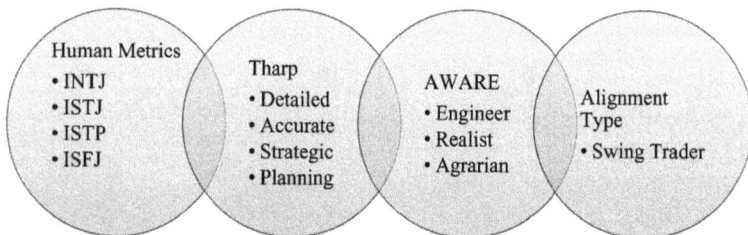

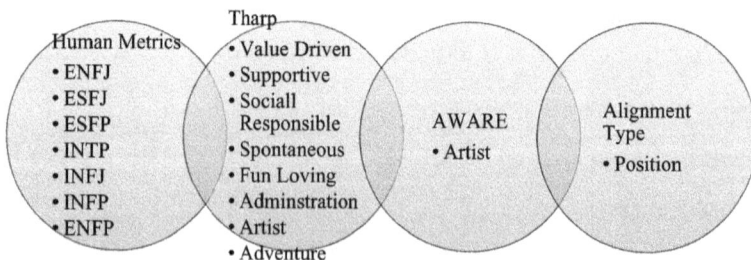

Human Metrics
- ENTP
- ISFP
- ESTP

Tharp
- Innovative
- Independent
- Accurate
- Spontaneous

AWARE
- Warrior
- Realist

Alignment Type
- Scalp Trader

Human Metrics
- ENTJ
- ESTJ

Tharp
- Administrative
- Facilitative
- Strategic
- Planning

AWARE
- Agrarian
- Realist

Alignment Type
- Day Trader

Human Metrics
- INTJ
- ISTJ
- ISTP
- ISFJ

Tharp
- Detailed
- Accurate
- Strategic
- Planning

AWARE
- Engineer
- Realist
- Agrarian

Alignment Type
- Swing Trader

Human Metrics
- ENFJ
- ESFJ
- ESFP
- INTP
- INFJ
- INFP
- ENFP

Tharp
- Value Driven
- Supportive
- Sociall Responsible
- Spontaneous
- Fun Loving
- Adminstration
- Artist
- Adventure

AWARE
- Artist

Alignment Type
- Position

Chapter Takeaway:

Unsuccessful traders' mindset and actions are responsible for their losses; these are usually brought on and ruled by fear or greed.

It takes time to change our learned habits.

Successful traders are those who are positive and manage fear, greed and have a positive outlook.

Fear and greed are adaptive behaviors or "conditioned" based on stimuli. The market is the stimulus that triggers our learned behavior.

Each trader is different and has different goals and dreams. With this, each trader brings their own personality, shadows, egos, and ideas to the trading desk.

To know your true self, understand your trading habits and personality, you must acknowledge the psychology of the persona and shadows as a part of trading loss and gains.

To have a trader's mindset, you must align and trade with the correct methods and systems based on your personality.

2
FOUNDATION

"Most people don't understand the process. They get frustrated by it.
Don't Be. Focus."

~ David Sikhosana ~

Learning structure is the key to learning how markets work in all financial markets. All markets are riddled with an altered mindset, fear, and greed with markets moving up, down—and when the mindset is unsure sideways. With this behavior, momentum legs are created which are the foundation for the Harmony and Fibonacci Equality Principles. They can be measurable and rep- etitious. We will look into how various indicators play a role in the structure.

This chapter covers primary, secondary foundation type and what structure can be traded based on the personality profile. We examine how to identify and if we have nothing else on the chart to predict price and stay ahead of it for an expected move. We will also examine the target projections.

Defining the Method

Having a solid method requires knowledge of only a few concepts when trading. Using any or a combination of price, time, mo- mentum, structure, supply/demand, and ratio analysis is needed if a trader plans to trade. Having these tools as a foundation will give us the technical edge needed and will lay out a road map to potential profitability. Any method traded must be repeatable, reproducible, and profitable. This shows the validity of a method. With an aligned mindset, this method accomplishes this feat.

Primary foundation

The Price is Right

"Don't make friends with the trend, make friends with each candlestick,"
~ Vivek Nair ~

Price is the transaction of a product or security from a willing buyer to a willing seller. If they agree on terms a transaction is made. Through buying and selling price movements of support-resistance and supply-demand are created. Some traders look at these concepts as similar in scope; however, I view them differently.

Price Formation

Price formation is a visual representation of a trader's psychological mindset and agreement. When there is an agreement between buyers and sellers, price moves in reflection to this agreement and it is noted by viewing the price action on the chart (figure 2).

When the transaction is over, the price closes during a specific period and another battle of transactions begins. This creates candlestick patterns within the market.

There are many ways to view this transaction from the Volume, Renko, Tick, Kagi, Dyno bars, and candlesticks. We will use candlestick as this is a standard across all trading platforms in tick format. Many traders use this format for analysis and confirmation. Below are examples of transactions and the final decisions made by closing the candle (figure 2.1-2.2). This pattern type suggests bullish activity and the other as bearish activity. We will only focus on a decision that produces engulfing patterns.

Figure 2 Representation of traders deciding.

Figure 2.1 Buyers in the market (Bullish Engulfing).

Figure 2.2 Sellers in the market (Bearish Engulfing).

Traders should have one or two strong indicators of a reversal. With added confirmation, one candle is all that is needed for a reversal. We will discuss engulfing reversal candles. This candle type is a strong indicator of buying and selling when aligned with SR-SD Zones and structure.

SR-SD Zones

Resistance is the amount of a product which sellers want to sell at a certain price point and support is the amount of a product which buyers want to buy at a certain price point. The transaction occurs in wick areas.

Supply Demand is different. Supply is the amount of a product or security which sellers want to sell at an exact price. Demand is the amount of a product or security which buyers want to buy at an exact price. Transactions occur in the open and close of a candle body.

As we make transactions, the price increases as buyers outnumber the sellers, and the price will decrease if sellers outnumber the buyers. Because of this continuous tug of war for better prices, SR-SD Zones are created.

This concept combines support-resistance with supply and demand. SR-SD zones can be static and dynamic. To capture and capitalize on a potential move, zones must be created and respected. Why not place an order at the exact or certain price? The trader may not get filled. By placing an order in a zone, the likelihood of it getting filled is high. Make sure we have the sign of a candle formation reversal when in the SR-SD zone.

Static SR-SD (Horizontal Lines)

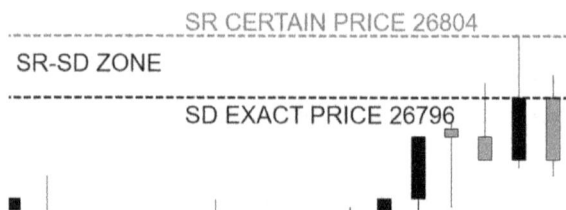

Figure 2.3 Example of Static SR-SD price area and zone.

Dynamic SR-SD (Trend Lines)

Figure 2.4 Example of Dynamic SR-SD price area and zone.

Building a House

To build a house, one must have a strong foundation. The learning of structure (wave structure) is the basic foundation of trading. As traders, we must understand how markets move if we are ever to achieve consistent profits.

The structure is a form of technical analysis, and it is seen all over the charts. A trader can be as simple or as complex in their analysis as necessary in making a decision.

The analysis will be focused on two types of markets. Bullish and Bearish wave structure. We do not trade sideways markets. If the current chart you are viewing is sideways, then no trade needs to be taken.

Structure Classification

How is wave structure classified? To determine if the structure has been confirmed, we look to the left to determine if the price has broken previous price structure. If price closes by 1 point, it is classified as a valid structure determination.

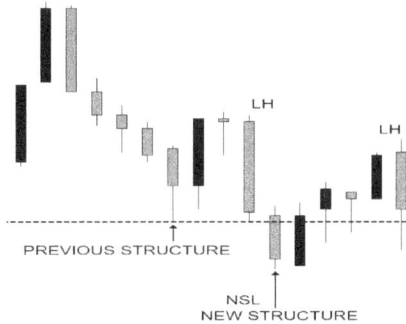

Figure 2.5 Example of structure classification.

Overall Direction

To trade, traders must have a road map to determine the direction for the trading day. Our map is structure. The structure can be identified as micro, minor, intermediate, and major.

This is in correlation to scalping, day, swing, and position trading. To trade successfully, we first must know our personality and be in correct alignment. The assessment test should have given guidance.

To be in structure alignment in the overall context, we first look at the current price to see where we are. We then look left and find structure at the highest high and the lowest low to the left not broken.

Those two points where the price is trapped are our direction classification for the day on the chart based on our trader personality.

Figure 2.6 Example of bullish price trap.

Figure 2.7 Example of bearish price trap.

Bullish Wave Structure

Bullish wave structure consists of a New Structure High and constructed as "NSH," followed by a higher low or "HL."

Figure 2.8 Bullish Wave Structure.

Bearish Wave Structure

Bearish wave structure comprising a New Structure Low and constructed as "NSL," followed by a lower high or "LH."

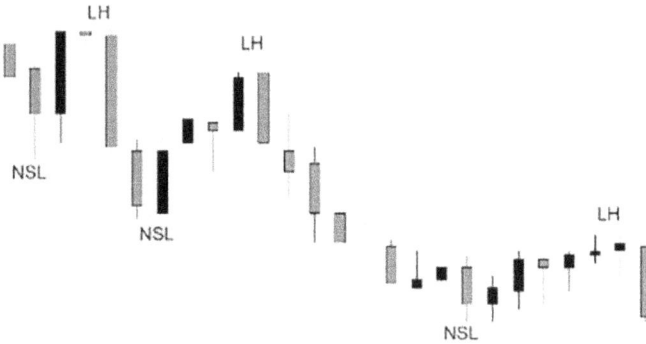

Figure 2.9 Bearish Wave Structure.

Learning this skill alone is enough to be profitable in the mar- kets. By understanding this sequence, it will give you an edge to expect the next move. Without this basic skill firmly embedded in your mindset, it is virtually impossible to move forward.

If you have found and identified your trader type, your focus should only be on the section(chapter 4) pertaining to your style and type then PRACTICE, PRACTICE, PRACTICE.

Once you have mastered this section, your eyes will be open to structure everywhere! Once you see it, it can't be unseen.

With this enlightenment, the first response will be to trade all structure on all timeframes. This would be a mistake. Stick to the trader type, and trade according to the sample trading crite- ria. Figure 2.10 shows different trader types. Which one are you designed to trade?

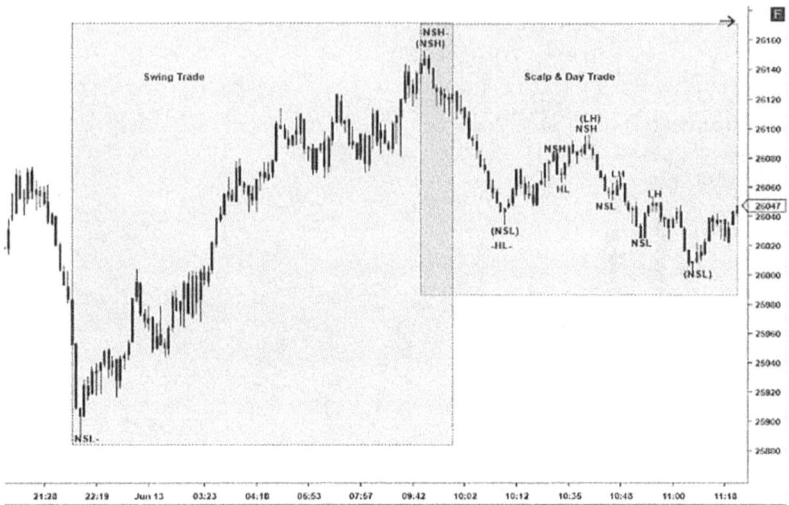

Figure 2.10 Trader Type based on Personality.

The Pattern

Once you have practice expecting the next move, the next logical progression is to learn and apply the pattern.

I will discuss two principles, Harmony and Fibonacci Equality. One or both could arrive at a stop-loss and projected target.

We see the pattern everywhere on the chart and it's a method using the recognition of specific wave structures that possess ratio alignments that quantify the pattern.

These patterns are recognized by the momentum "leg" of the previous price wave to identify a probable target or termination point on the markets.

Once momentum has been identified, you can exit a position based upon the expectation that the same historic price will occur.

By industry standards, we have given patterns multiple names Bat, Butterfly, Gartley, Cypher, etc. This approach will be different. It's harmony in the markets. Harmonics are having a symbiotic relationship with price.

Pattern Principles

Two pattern principles can arrive at a trading decision. Harmony and Fibonacci Equality. Using momentum leg, we plot the close price to gain a more accurate depiction.

For every correction, there should be a wave structure equal in its measure. Most traders know this pattern as AB=CD or ABCD.

In the Market Harmony Principle, the Fibonacci sequence is not part of the projection target point, but in Fibonacci Equality, we utilize ratios in the second principle. To increase the higher probability of success, I have changed the Fibonacci ratios.

To conclude, in historical chart analysis these two principals have yielded favorable results for its projection targets and they have respected price for their reversal points and their projection target in Fibonacci Equality.

If plotted at the close of price, it should hit the target before rejection occurs.

Market Harmony Principle

To arrive at such a conclusion, we will utilize a harmony principle example.

In figure 2.11, we identified the NSH of price. We apply momentum "leg line" to price structure to determine the potential direction. We use line charts as the focus on close of price.

Once a correction has been identified, we attach a copy of the same leg line to the correction. We switch back to candlestick tick chart to observe the price action.

We should achieve harmony. That's it! The market has harmony, or it doesn't. Here, the price completed the pattern to the point then reversed.

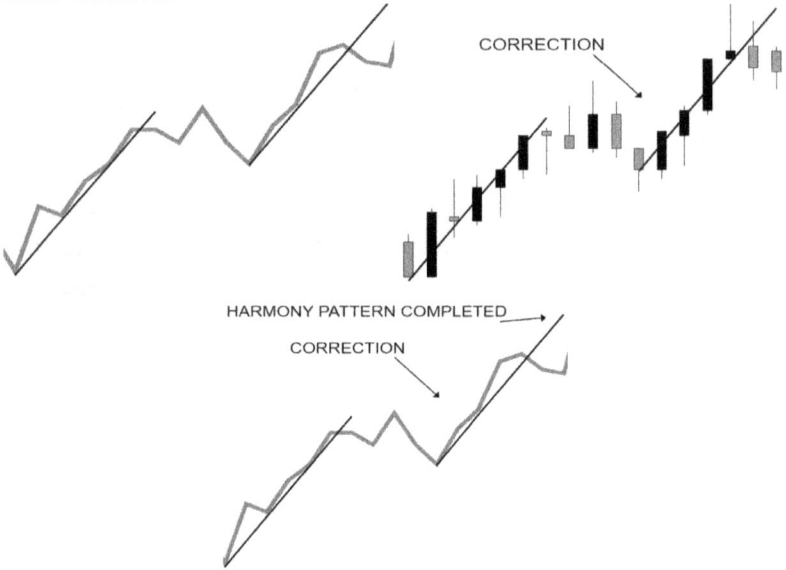

Figure 2.11 Example of harmony in action.

Fibonacci Equality Principle

Their many books researched regarding the Fibonacci Equality Prin- ciple. The Fibonacci Principle is based on geometric shapes starting as far back as Egypt with Pythagoras, the father of Geometry.

This principle then migrated into Italy and was rediscovered by Leonardo de Pisa. The principle is known and found all around us in the universe and we apply this popular technical tool and concept in trading as well.

Fibonacci Equality Principle uses the same concepts as others; however, the ratio has been changed for better efficiency to determine the entry and exit point.

The traditional (classic) Fibonacci template will not be used. I show the ratio settings below.

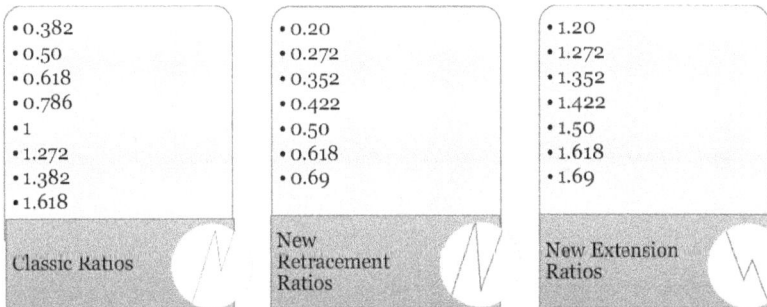

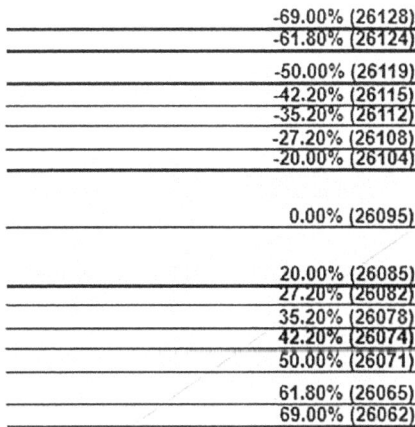

Classic Ratios	New Retracement Ratios	New Extension Ratios
• 0.382	• 0.20	• 1.20
• 0.50	• 0.272	• 1.272
• 0.618	• 0.352	• 1.352
• 0.786	• 0.422	• 1.422
• 1	• 0.50	• 1.50
• 1.272	• 0.618	• 1.618
• 1.382	• 0.69	• 1.69
• 1.618		

```
-69.00% (26128)
-61.80% (26124)
-50.00% (26119)
-42.20% (26115)
-35.20% (26112)
-27.20% (26108)
-20.00% (26104)

 0.00% (26095)

20.00% (26085)
27.20% (26082)
35.20% (26078)
42.20% (26074)
50.00% (26071)

61.80% (26065)
69.00% (26062)
```

Figure 2.12 Visual Example of New Fibonacci ratios used.

Once the Fibonacci sequence is set up, place it on any wave structure point and notice where the retracement happens and where it ends.

Most traders place their Fibonacci retracements at the wicks; however, before the price hits the wicks and reverses, it will AL-WAYS hit price first (figure 2.13).

The price closed and reversed at the 35.20% market 26,151, so according to the Fibonacci Equality Principle, the projected target should be the 35.20% extension, 26,184 which calculates to be 33 ticks.

As a side note, once price breaks and closes for a new structure high, there is a high win rate of taking profit at 20% extension. We achieved the target to the point and then reversed before hitting or overall Market Harmony target.

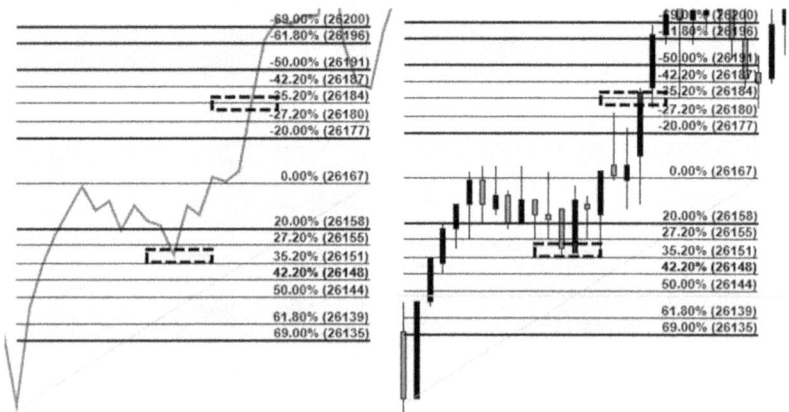

Figure 2.13 Example of New Fibonacci ratios applied to a line chart.

In using ratios, we will not always get a "perfect bounce" off a certain line. We use this in combination with other tools to strengthen the resolve in our trading decision.

Secondary foundation

Just in Time

It's about timing. All trades are not good trades. Time selection is key to entering a trade. Since we look to enter wave structure bullish or bearish patterns, we have to realize timing is important.

Using oscillators helps us realize the price is running out of steam and becoming exhaustive in either an overbought or over- sold situation and it is time to watch for an opportunity.

Any oscillator that shows these conditions is valid in this method. I have been using the relative spread strength (RSS) indicator for timing.

If we use anything other than what is used with this method, we assume all risk associated with this decision.

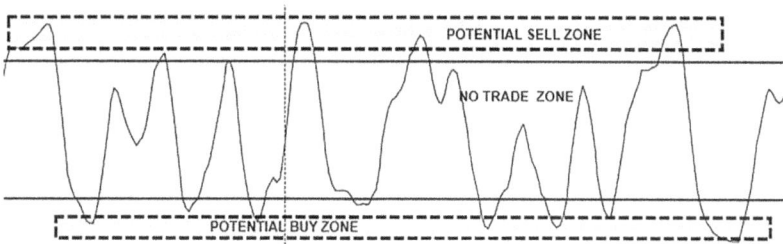

Figure 2.14 Example of finding the timing.

May the Force Be with You

Moving averages are indicators used to help determine how much momentum there is in a security. Also, it helps a trader to stay with the trend and on the correct side of the market.

The stronger the angle, the stronger the momentum. Traders seek to visualize this when any moving average is on the chart.

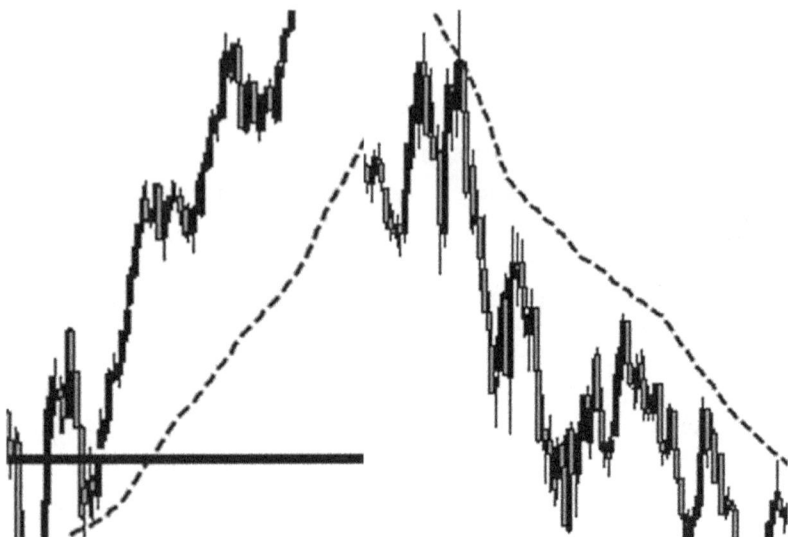

Figure 2.15 Example of momentum force.

Yesterday

This should be a straightforward concept for most of you. If the price is above the previous day high, a trader must look to buy. If the price is below the previous day low, then a trader must look to sell. If the price remains in the middle, then a trader does

BUY ABOVE LINE

DO NOTHING IN LINE

SELL BELOW LINE

Figure 2.16 Example of Previous high or low determination.

Chapter Takeaway:

Primary foundations use core concept as wave structure, SR-SD zones, and price formation to decide.

Wave structure comprises NSH to HL in a bullish market and NSL to LH in a seller's market.

SR-SD Zones are buying and selling areas once confirmed by an engulfing candle.

The secondary foundation is optional but suggestive.

3
MANAGEMENT

"All statistics have outliers. Money management, therefore, is key to the process of good trading."

~ Yvan Byeajee ~

Money Management

The best way to protect your capital is to have the mindset of a money manager and preserve your capital at all costs. Managers deal with risk controls and odds analysis.

For success to occur, we must apply sound money principles and a refocusing should be enacted if one has gone astray.

One Percent

The most sound principles are always to use a stop-loss and allocate a small position to the trade as little as 1%.

Each trading style carries its own stress and risk tolerance. No matter the capital available in your trading account, it should remain at 1% of the total account until the material in this book is understood to its fullest.

The best way to achieve this aim is to trade the MYM micro mini Dow futures, which equates to 0.50 cents per tick.

This removes the conditioned mindset and only focuses on the concept of the method. This should give you more room to relax and enhance your newfound trading knowledge.

Risk-Reward Ratio (RRR)

Risk-Reward Ratio is a philosophy you should have as part of a sound management strategy.

Placing stop-loss at the level described in this book should give you at least a 1:1 ratio. Anything more would increase risk and skew the ratio and increase risk tolerance.

Trade Management

Entry

When submitting an order, the market will tell you if it wants to move in your predetermined direction, so it is advisable to place a stop market order 2 ticks away.

Stop-loss Placement

Stop-loss placement should always be significant and not arbitrary. Once criteria have been met, we must place stop orders 2 ticks beyond the wicks or at the next Fibonacci line beyond wicks.

Wicks? Yes. It is understandable that we are discussing price, but it's for price projections. Wicks are rejection points (zones), and it is advisable to be out of reach of rejection areas.

Knowing Market Harmony and Fibonacci Equality gives us an edge to placement. It takes the guesswork out of the entry, stop-loss, and targets.

Figure 2.17 Example of Entry, Stop-loss, and Target.

Chapter Takeaway:

Each trading style carries its own stress and risk tolerance.

We always use the best money management principle, a stop-loss, and allocate as little as one percent to the trading position.

4
TRADER SYNTHESIS

"In Zen, we strive to bring both the mind and the body into perfect combination so that there is no intrinsic difference between them."

~ Frederick Lenz ~

To bring things into perspective, we must combine the things we have learned. Each phase of the trader type process will have its own trade plan, management rules. Each type has it owns risk tolerance rules.

We will show trade criteria examples with a step-by-step process you should use to decide.

If you decide not to use this trading method, you must back and forward test any method for validity and accuracy.

Please refer to your trader alignment test for guidance on trader type.

Figure 2.18 Screenshot of each trader type.

Scalp Trader (micro trend)

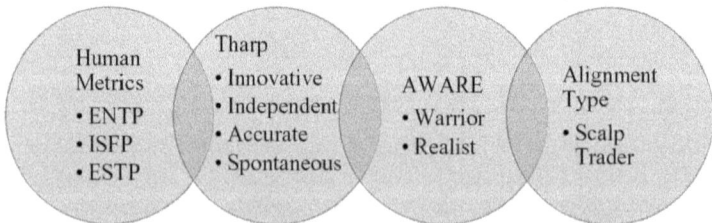

Human Metrics
- ENTP
- ISFP
- ESTP

Tharp
- Innovative
- Independent
- Accurate
- Spontaneous

AWARE
- Warrior
- Realist

Alignment Type
- Scalp Trader

Scalping is a trading method in which a trader seeks to achieve 3-4 ticks out of the market each time we enter a position. Be careful not to over trade.

One positive trade each day is the goal. Three ticks will be the minimum projected target. I will execute trades on the 89-tick chart.

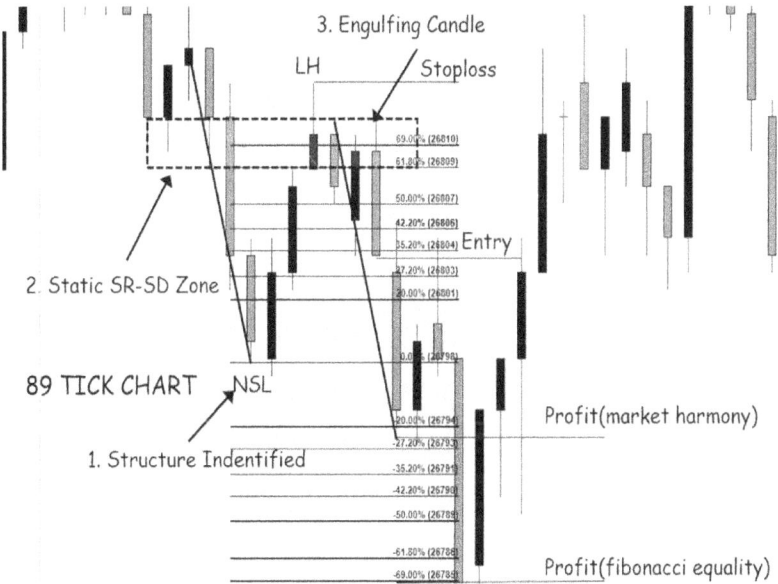

Figure 2.19 Example of 89 tick sell criteria

In figure 2.19, we first identified a new structure low (NSL). This is a sign the market wants to move lower.

According to sell wave structure, you should wait for a lower high (LH) to form. The market moved up and created a lower high (LH) into SR-SD Zone.

Now that we are in the SR-SD Zone, we must wait for rejection out of the zone and form an engulfing candle. Once we recognize this, enter 2 ticks below the signal candle 26,804.

We must place the stop-loss 2 ticks above lower high 26,816. This is a risk of 12 ticks. We achieved profit 26,793 (11 ticks) using Market Harmony. If we decided on Fibonacci Equality, we would achieve 26,785 (31 ticks).

Day Trader (minor trend)

Day Trading exploits a minor trend structure in which we seek to achieve 7-19 ticks out of the market each time we enter a position. Seven ticks will be the minimum projected target. The 173 tick chart will be the trading timeframe of choice.

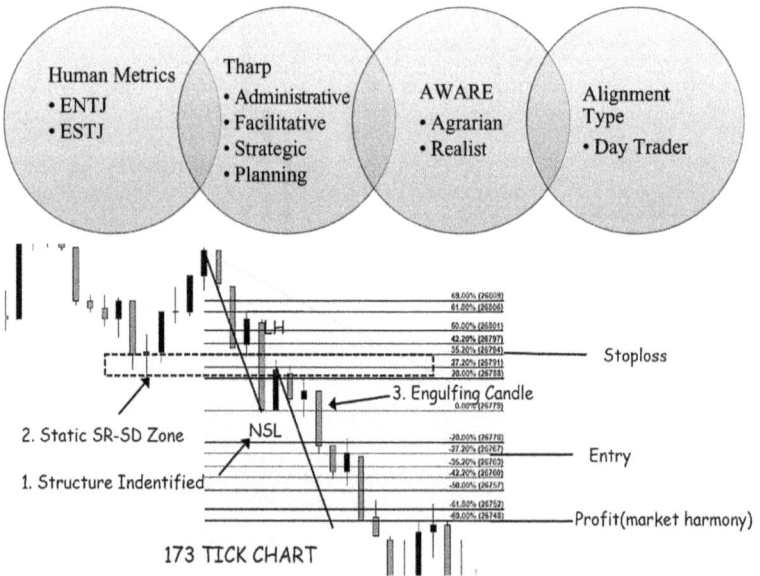

Figure 2.20 Example of 173 tick sell criteria

In the 173 tick chart (figure 2.20), a new structure low (NSL) arrived. This is a sign that the market wants to move lower, but we have to wait for a correction.

Then, the market moved up and created a lower high (LH) in the static SR-SD Zone. Now we must wait for rejection out of the zone signified by an engulfing candle.

Entry was 26,765 and stop-loss is 26,794. Risk is 29 ticks.

We achieved profit using Market Harmony 26,748 of 17 ticks.

Swing Trader (intermediate trend)

Swing Trader exploits intermediate trend structure in which a trader seeks to achieve 69-275 ticks out of the market each time we enter a position. Sixty-nine ticks will be the minimum projected target.

The 1597 tick chart will be the trading timeframe of choice. All criteria are exact on the day trade chart with secondary criteria of exhaustion on timing (figure 2.21). The timing was not there on the first candle but was on the second.

Entry is 24,886 and stop-loss is 25,001. This a risk of 115 ticks. We achieved Market Harmony profit of 24,661 (225 ticks), and if we used Fibonacci Equality, the profit achieved was 24,748 (138ticks).

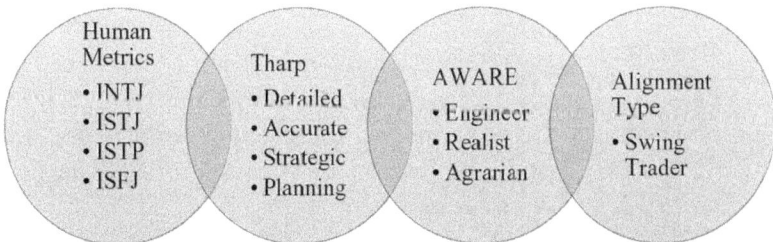

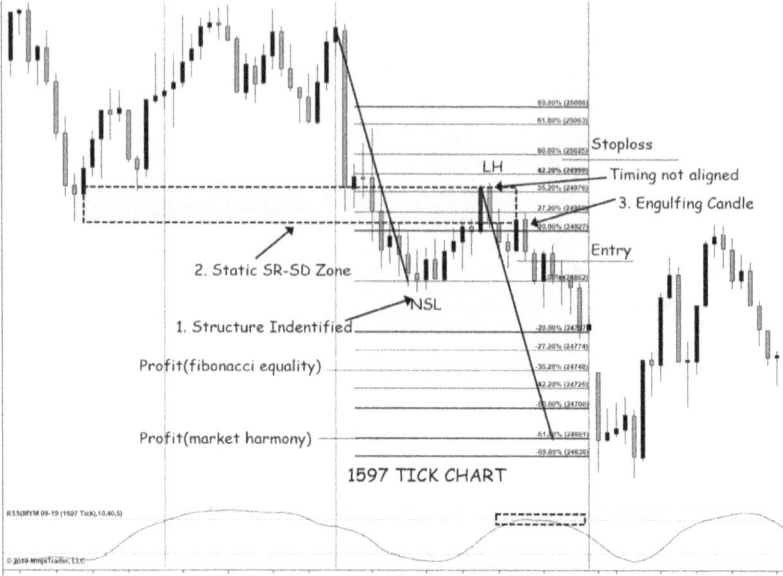

Figure 2.21 Example of 1597 tick sell criteria

Position Trader (major trend)

Position traders exploit a major trend structure in which a trader seeks to achieve 293-500 ticks out of the market each time they enter a position.

The minimum projected target will be 293 ticks. The 2000 tick chart will be the trading timeframe of choice.

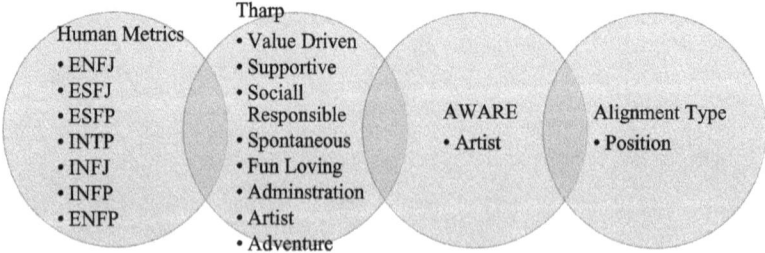

Human Metrics	Tharp		
• ENFJ	• Value Driven		
• ESFJ	• Supportive		
• ESFP	• Sociall Responsible	AWARE	Alignment Type
• INTP	• Spontaneous	• Artist	• Position
• INFJ	• Fun Loving		
• INFP	• Adminstration		
• ENFP	• Artist		
	• Adventure		

Figure 2.22 Example of 2000 tick buy criteria fell short of both targets.

The market moved from a seller's market new structure low (NSL) to a buyer new structure high (NSH). Now we have to wait for a higher low (HL) to arrive in the SR-SD Zone.

Bullish candle signaled, and we placed a stop market order for 25,657 and Stop-loss at 25,497. This is a risk of 160 ticks. This trade was a loss as neither target was hit because of dynamic SR-SD Zone. It also signaled the oscillator. Criteria for a sell was identified and would have been a 385 tick win, making up for the 160 tick loss.

Trade Criteria

BUY IF:

It must meet the primary conditions:

1. Have we identified a New Wave Structure High?
2. If it creates an NSH, then wait for a correction into the static SR-SD zone.
3. Is there an engulfing candle in an area of SR-SD?
4. Enter a buy-stop market 2 points above the engulfing candle. Position stop-loss 2 points below signal candle or at the Fibonacci line.
5. Project Harmony move using Fibonacci Equality or momentum wave of the previous move of price.
6. Take profit at Harmony/Fibonacci termination point or profit target.

Secondary *(optional but suggestive)*

7. Oscillator – Is it oversold?
8. Moving Average – Does MA has a strong angle force to the upside?
9. Previous HL – Is it above yesterday's high?
10. Trend Line – Are we bouncing off Dynamic SR-SD Zone?

SELL IF:

It must meet the primary conditions:

1. Has a New Wave Structure Low been identified?
2. If it creates an NSL, then wait for a correction into static SR-SD zone.
3. Is there an engulfing candle in an area of SR-SD?
4. Enter a sell-stop market 2 ticks below the engulfing candle. Position stop-loss 2 points above a signal candle or at the Fibonacci line.
5. Project Harmony move using Fibonacci or momentum wave of the previous move of price.

6. Take profit at Harmony, Fibonacci termination point or profit target.

Secondary *(optional but suggestive)*

7. Oscillator – Is it overbought?
8. Moving Average – Does MA has a strong angle force to the downside?
9. Previous HL – Is it below yesterday's low?
10. Trend Line – Are we bouncing off Dynamic SR-SD Zone?

Third-Party Software

To make the structure easier to view, I subscribe to a third party software program which looks into a candle and price called Dyno bars. Standard Renko works well also and its free. I have found it to be easier to view structure, but as with anything, finding the right timeframe is key to using any program.

I am not recommending or endorsing this I am only suggest- ing what I use occasionally and disclosing there are more ways to trade. I am always on the hunt for simplicity. I don't sug- gest spending money you don't have. It is not cheap, and it renews every year. THIS BOOK HAS WHAT YOU NEED!

Dyno bars

Trading these bars is the same as the primary foundation. The only thing we look for is this:

Buy Criteria (opposite for sell):

Price above yesterday high.
A cross of 14-50 SMA.

First Candle correction into 14-50 SMA and does not close beyond 50 SMA.

A bullish return.

Enter 2 points above.

Take Profit at 13.7% extension or let it ride!

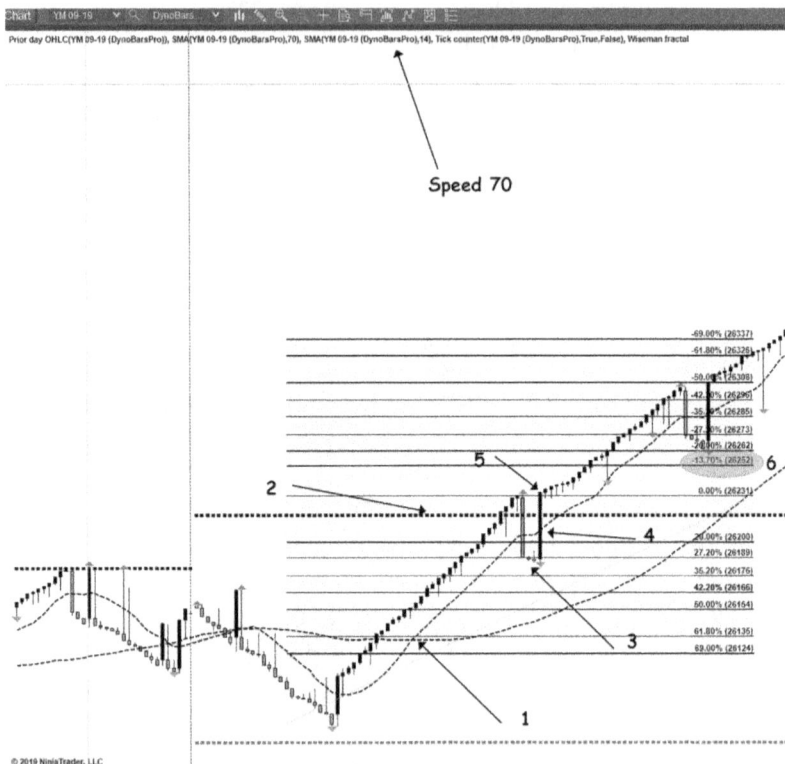

Chapter Takeaway:

To keep the mindset relaxed and aligned, it is best to trade your personality.

Trade criteria offer specific rules for entering and exiting a trade.

5
RETIREMENT

"Retirement, a time to do what you want to do, when you want to do it, where you want to do it and how you want to do it."

~ *Catherine Pulsifer* ~

Retirement Control

How do you take control of your finances? It is about aligning the mindset, the method, and sound money management.

The overarching theme to getting rid of gurus and gaining control is to achieve a better annual percentage rate (APR) on deposit in your bank account or return on your investment of your 401K.

If you can do this, you can fire them and take control of your own financial life.

As you have gotten comfortable trading your newfound concept and are consistent, diversification should enter your mind.

Diversification

How can a trader multiply their efforts? By spreading the wealth around in different accounts. This was always the goal for me once I found a consistent method of trading, so I will share what I have done.

Realize factors will be different so you must consult the brokerage house to see if they offer this service, if not, fire them and move to one that suits your needs.

NinjaTrader Brokerage is where trading takes place. To date, there are two places where futures account will need to be open, Dorman Trading or Phillips. I am with Dorman.

These companies are clearing houses (settlement) where the money will move through. We must set up an account with them to use NinjaTrader's platform.

You need to open a Midland IRA. This is a self-directed retirement vehicle you can use. But to do so, you will first have to set up an account with them.

There is a setup fee incurred. You could transfer your old retirement account over to Midland. Allocate an amount to trade on NinjaTrader's platform.

Once you have made a profit, you can transfer it back to the retirement account. For my account, the overall achievement is 15% on each account per year.

Every year starting January 1st three accounts, two self-directed IRAs and one trading account get funded to the maximum contribution. I calculate the total and calculate 15% for the year and write it out on my trading board.

Why give it a year? It stops me from over trading, taking unnecessary positions or forcing trades which are not in alignment. In this way, I can trade without stress.

My job isn't to fight the market only to take part in it to reach the goal. That's it. This percentage goal does not include the cost of inflation.

Now, let's put things into context. Let's say you have the amount below at retirement. This would be your yearly income not including taxes. This will show you how much you need to save if you achieve the same goal.

$$\$250,000 \times 15\% = \$37,500 \text{ per year}$$

$$\$62,500 \times 15\% = \$9,375 \text{ per year}$$

$$\$31,250 \times 15\% = \$4,687.50 \text{ per year}$$

If you save the right capital, 15% is a good living after you retire. Think about what would happen if you stopped contributing and only used the amount above. Your initial investment would never be touched. That's true freedom and enough to get out of the **RAT TRAP** and **BREAK FREE!**

6

PUT UP OR SHUT UP

*"The focus should not be on talking. Talk is cheap.
It must be on action."*

~ Howard Berman ~

I executed real positions to show the validity of the method. These results are not typical.

Live Trade Examples

Market Traded
YM (Dow)
Platform: Ninja trader Brokerage (NT8)

Goal: One trade day on trader type base on time and market conditions.

Indicators used:

RSS:10,40,3
MA:14-50 SMA,9 EMA (displacement 2)
Previous Day HL Fibonacci(modified)
Tick counter Renko:18-1
Dynobars software package

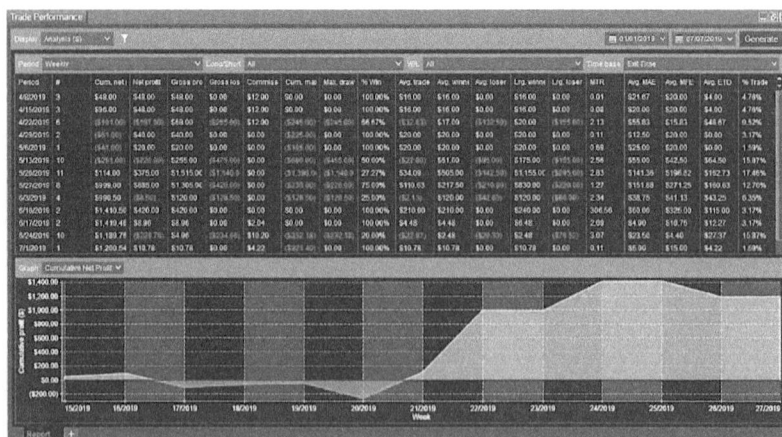

Period	#	Cum. net	Net profit	Gross pro	Gross los	Commiss	Cum. max	Max. draw	% Win	Avg. trade	Avg. winni	Avg. loser	Lrg. winni	Lrg. loser	MFR	Avg. MAE	Avg. MFE	Avg. ETD	% Trade
4/8/2019	3	$48.00	$48.00	$48.00	$0.00	$12.00	$0.00	$0.00	100.00%	$16.00	$16.00	$0.00	$16.00	$0.00	0.01	$21.67	$20.00	$4.80	4.78%
4/15/2019	3	$96.00	$48.00	$48.00	$0.00	$12.00	$0.00	$0.00	100.00%	$16.00	$16.00	$0.00	$16.00	$0.00	0.04	$20.00	$20.00	$4.80	4.78%
4/22/2019	6	($61.00)	($197.50)	$69.00	($266.50)	$12.00	($246.00)	($245.00)	66.67%	($12.43)	$17.00	($112.50)	$20.00	($115.00)	2.13	$55.83	$15.83	$48.67	0.52%
4/29/2019	2	($61.00)	$45.00	$45.00	$0.00	$6.00	($235.00)	$0.00	100.00%	$20.00	$20.00	$3.00	$20.00	$0.00	0.11	$12.50	$20.00	$0.80	3.17%
5/6/2019	1	($41.00)	$20.00	$20.00	$0.00	$0.00	($155.00)	$0.00	100.00%	$20.00	$20.00	$0.00	$20.00	$0.00	0.86	$25.00	$20.00	$0.80	1.59%
5/13/2019	10	($291.00)	($250.00)	$295.00	($475.00)	$0.00	($690.00)	($445.00)	50.00%	($22.80)	$51.00	($96.00)	$175.00	($155.00)	2.56	$55.00	$42.50	$64.50	15.87%
5/20/2019	11	$114.00	$375.00	$1,515.00	($1,140.00)	$0.00	($1,390.00)	($1,140.00)	27.27%	$34.09	$365.00	($342.50)	$1,155.00	($595.00)	2.83	$143.39	$198.82	$192.73	17.46%
5/27/2019	6	$999.00	$885.00	$1,305.00	($420.00)	$0.00	($235.00)	($220.00)	75.09%	$119.83	$217.50	($210.00)	$830.00	($220.00)	1.27	$151.88	$271.25	$160.63	12.70%
6/3/2019	4	$990.50	($8.50)	$120.00	($128.50)	$0.00	($128.50)	($128.50)	25.00%	($2.13)	$120.00	($342.65)	$120.00	($66.00)	2.34	$38.75	$41.13	$43.25	6.35%
6/10/2019	2	$1,410.50	$420.00	$420.00	$0.00	$0.00	$0.00	$0.00	100.00%	$210.00	$210.00	$0.00	$240.00	$0.00	306.56	$60.00	$325.00	$115.00	3.17%
6/17/2019	2	$1,410.46	$8.96	$8.96	$0.00	$2.04	$0.00	$0.00	100.00%	$4.48	$4.48	$0.00	$6.48	$0.00	2.08	$4.90	$10.75	$12.27	3.17%
6/24/2019	10	$1,189.78	($320.76)	$4.96	($334.66)	$10.20	($352.18)	($332.13)	20.69%	($22.87)	$2.48	($329.50)	$2.48	($374.53)	3.07	$23.56	$4.46	$27.37	15.87%
7/1/2019	1	$1,200.54	$10.78	$10.76	$0.00	$4.22	($321.40)	$0.00	100.00%	$10.78	$10.78	$0.00	$10.78	$0.00	0.11	$6.90	$15.00	$4.22	1.59%

7
CONCLUSION

Congratulations are in order for learning a new way to view and engage the financial markets to break free.

I realize we have gone over many things in the book. For most of you, the concepts will be straightforward, but for others, it may take time to develop the skills. It is okay.

Anything that will be of value in your lives takes time and effort, but once the skill materializes, it is with you forever. Take your time and don't rush. So, what do we do now?

Before trading begins, we must have the direction, a trader's mindset, and the trader must align with the correct methods and systems based on their personality. The market is the stimulus that triggers our learned behavior.

To achieve this, we must understand our conditioned behavior and how fear and greed are adaptive behaviors or "conditioned" based on stimuli.

The trading method uses primary foundations as core concepts using wave structure, SR-SD zones, and price formation to decide.

Wave structure comprises new structure high (NSH) to higher low (HL) in a bullish market and a new structure low (NSL) to lower high (LH) in a seller's market.

SR-SD zones are buying and selling areas once confirmed by an engulfing candle. If you can grasp these primary concepts, this is the only tool you will need for success.

For further confirmation, we use the secondary foundation, though optional it is suggestive for added success.

The key point of it all is master the mindset and wave structure. If you are looking for the holy grail, this isn't it.

First, if you can control your mind (shadows) and identify structure while trading, you have mastered trading. With a strong mindset, you can trade any method and be profitable.

Second, wave structure identification. Depending on what time frame you are viewing, the structure will show itself. It is different for every time frame.

Techniques:

> Visualization Techniques – Before opening your trading computer, sit with your eyes closed and visualize yourself trading. Visualize using all the new tools learned, putting a stop-loss, setting targets in a proper and logical place, identifying the structure, SR-SD Zones. It will get easier.

> Simulation Training – On the weekend use this time to perform a mock trade. Turn on the simulator and watch price move and at each time ask yourself, "Is this a NSH? If so, I should expect the price to move down and achieve a higher low in the SR-SD Zone." This will get you familiar with expecting moves. Stay ahead of price.

With the tools learned and gained, you can take control of your financial future. Here are quotes that helped me along the way:

QUOTES:

1. "Trade only when the market is bullish or bearish."
2. "Do not trade every day."
3. "Only enter a trade after the action of the market confirms your opinion and then enter."

4. "Buy when stocks reach a new high. Sell short when they reach a new low."

5. "Wishful thinking must be banished."

6. "Big movements take time to develop."

7. Patterns repeat because human nature hasn't changed for thousands of years."

8. "Money is made by sitting, not trading."

9. "It takes time to make money."

10. "It was never my thinking made the big money for me, it always was sitting."

11. "Nobody can catch all the fluctuations.

12. "The desire for constant action irrespective of underlying conditions is responsible for many losses in Wall Street even among the professionals, who feel that they must take home some money every day, as though they were working for regular wages."

13. "Buy right, sit tight."

Thanks for reading! Please add a short review and let me know what you think after the method is applied.

REFERENCES

Jung, C. G. (1969). *Psychology and religion: West and East.*
Princeton, NJ: Princeton University Press.
Skinner, B. (1960). *Science and human behavior.*
New York: Mc Millan Company.

APPENDIX

Human Metrics
http://www.humanmetrics.com/personality

Tharp Test
http://www.tharptradertest.com

Market Psychology
http://tests.marketpsych.com/personality_test.php

AWARE Test
http://www.daytradingpsychology.com/

Ninja Trader Brokerage
http://www.ninjatrader.com/

Midland IRA
http://www.midlandira.com/

AUTHOR SECTION

James began his journey in finance and trader education on accident. He as many others lost all his retirement and saving in the 2008 financial crisis.

Through his frustration and anger, he took his finances into his own hands and learn everything he could to control his own financial future.

His road was difficult and financial loss through learning continued. The journey took a positive turn once he applied the basics of what money, investing and trading is and developed basic simple concepts.

He found his passion for teaching and assisting people with their journey to take their power back into their own hands through financial education, trading concepts to invest in the YM Dow futures and MYM Dow futures derivatives markets.

www.ingramcontent.com/pod-product-compliance
Lightning Source LLC
Chambersburg PA
CBHW031909200326

41597CB00012B/555